HOW TO ANSWER

DIFFICULT QUESTIONS

WHEN SELLING

Be prepared –
Don`t get caught

JOHN MEPHAM

ISBN: 13:978-1499388039
Copyright @ 2014 John Mepham

ABOUT THE AUTHOR

I joined a firm of estate agents and auctioneers when leaving school. After gaining valuable experience in the property business I became a partner in a well-established firm of estate agents.

My connections with certain business associates led to me being offered the position of Managing Director of a public property company with a quote on the London Stock Exchange. Always being willing to go the next step up the career ladder I willingly accepted. I held that post for some twenty-two years.

Until my retirement I was a Chartered Surveyor.

During all my years in the tough property world I have negotiated at the highest level and drafted hundreds of advertisements that successfully did their job. Therefore, without doubt, I have the experience and knowledge to put this book before you.

JOHN MEPHAM

FOREWORD:

When reading this book you will soon realise that you are regarded as the seller. Therefore, the words "you" and "yours" always denote a seller.

The answers given in this book are to demonstrate that even the most difficult questions, which aim to trap the seller into condemning himself out of his own mouth, can be answered in a positive vain. The answers given are by way of a guide and will get the reader`s thoughts moving in the right direction. It will soon be realised that no question is all good or all bad; each one must be treated as being dangerous and answered positively. The reader will soon be composing his own answers from this helpful material.

THE FIRST VITAL LESSON THAT YOU MUST LEARN AND NEVER FORGET WHEN SELLING

Even the most simple and innocent sounding question that you are likely to hear has an ulterior motive - often a well-hidden one - and is trying to extract an item of information that will be of important assistance to the questioner as negotiations proceed. That is the reason why you must always be on your guard and exercise caution when replying. A mere slip of the tongue or a careless aside could weaken both the chance of selling and the price likely to be obtained. That would be a big plus to the potential buyer and a big minus to you.

You will frequently be asked some questions that are impossible to honestly answer without, in some way or other, divulging information that may completely or partially ruin your line of reasoning. Often the question is posed by an aggressive/cunning opponent who is keen to show off superior negotiating powers. When faced with such a tricky person tread cautiously as the real purpose of the question is to gain a distinct advantage. In fact, treat all questions with that warning in mind. There is no hiding place and you cannot remain silent. Of course, there is always the reply that the question cannot be answered for a personal, commercial or similar reason. That answer hints that there may be something being hidden and the questioner will make you feel uncomfortable by probing further.

Some examples of types of questions mentioned in the last paragraph are within the fifteen questions in this book. The answers are the writer's suggestions. You may have other ideas and come up with different (and better!) answers. One of the aims of this book is to help readers to answer or - like politicians - to sidestep too probing questions without compromising their own position. The reader must learn not to be condemned out of his own mouth. It is such an easy trap to fall into.

You must immediately dismiss an offensive question. Such questions may be personal, contain vulgar, rude or foul language, be racial, political or of a religious nature. The most harmful defence is to answer in the same mood as the questioner. Wouldn't you just love to do so? Beware, without doubt that will cause a nasty controversy...and that will get you nowhere. So, how do you deal with that dilemma?

You may well feel that it is pointless trying to bargain with such an obnoxious individual. When such an occasion arises you will have to decide whether to walk away or stand and reason. It depends on the conditions at the time and the extent to which you really want to complete a deal with him. The more that you want to buy or sell an item will govern the amount of unreasonable behaviour that you are prepared to tolerate. If you walk away make it absolutely clear why you are doing so. Show that it is his fault, not yours.

If you are keen to do business you must, of course, engage with that unpleasant character, although his attitude has made you thoroughly dislike him. Sadly, beggars cannot be choosers and whatever he does or says you must keep to the rules of the game and continue to sell yourself as a reasonable and friendly person. That is not easy to do - but, you must try. You say, "Come on now, Mr Brown, you are too nice a person to say that. Let's be reasonable...", or, "I didn't expect that our meeting would start like this. Let's start again and be polite to each other". If he does not calm down you have to be more forthright and say, "I am sorry to have to say that I am not used to such bad manners at a business meeting. If we cannot continue in a calmer atmosphere I will have to discontinue our discussions". These quotations can be altered to suit individual cases. The last comment may calm him...you may even get an apology. That should put you on your guard! Isn't that approach/defence better than entering a slanging match? In fact, there is no other option if you wish to conclude a successful deal.

The fifteen questions are typical ones likely to be asked in an everyday seller/buyer situation. They may not be put to you in the precise wording used. In fact, so often the question is hidden in a statement. Thereby hangs a hidden danger. The statement must not be allowed to remain as a fact accepted by you. That could be to your detriment. It must be immediately corrected or, at least, favourably commented upon.

It is essential to be as wary of a statement as you are - or, should be - of a direct (difficult) question. Never immediately take a statement at its face value as being true. Be suspicious; be on guard. A statement may contain a grain of truth. Be careful of the half-truth, you may believe and act upon the wrong half. As an example, see question number fourteen - "I'm lowering my offer". It is a statement but how many difficult questions does it pose? It will be helpful to ascertain **why** the agreed price is to be reduced before you are told the actual price reduction. Then, you will be in a better position to deal with that difficult of all aspects of selling - the person who tries to back down on an agreed price.

It is said that one should never say "never". That may be so; nevertheless here is a "never" that must always be obeyed. Never tell a lie, particularly when answering a question. There is no advantage whatsoever to be gained by telling a lie. There are both moral and legal reasons why a lie must never be uttered. As you consider the fifteen questions it will soon be realised that a truthful answer is the only way to have a successful deal. If a lie is told the liar will soon be rumbled and exposed as someone who cannot be trusted and - more dangerous to the liar - he will be avoided like the plague. When caught - note the word "when" not "if" - a profound apology is unlikely to end the sad episode. Like an elephant the person lied to will never forget. Once tarnished as a liar the damage is irreparable. To emphasise the danger, do remember that to be caught in such a disastrous predicament is likely to wreck the liar's cause. That is poetical justice.

*   *   *   *   *   *

Before considering the answers to the fifteen questions it will be beneficial to examine some of the general principles that govern the answering of questions in a competitive environment. Read and digest each of the following principles carefully and you will soon have a good background knowledge when you read and consider the fifteen difficult questions.

LISTEN CAREFULLY TO THE QUESTION

It is crucial that the real meaning of the question is either not missed or wrongly construed. For you to answer a question that has not been asked indicates a careless attitude. The questioner will pounce on that disability, consider that you are a poor salesperson and gain a profitable plus. His confidence will rise. So, always give the questioner the floor; listen carefully and do not interrupt. Ignore unrelated comments. How can you correctly answer a question that you have misheard because you did not bother to listen? You cannot do so. It is like trying to sink a twenty foot putt at golf...blindfolded.

IF YOU DO NOT CLEARLY UNDERSTAND THE QUESTION, SAY SO

If it is considered that the question is either unclear or ambiguous, apologise and ask for a clarification. That action must be taken or, as above, the wrong question may be answered. Few questioners are likely to be offended if their question is not understood. By apologising it will seem that it is your fault and not his. However, if needs be it is far better to upset the questioner than to do yourself some disservice by giving a wayward answer. There is no loss of self-esteem by asking the questioner to be clearer. It shows that you are alert and want to give a clear honest answer.

AN IRRELEVANT QUESTION SHOULD BE CHALLENGED

Do not hesitate to suggest that the question does not seem to have any bearing on the matter in hand. Will the questioner, please, state why it is relevant? Always endeavour to get such a question out of the way without delay. Do not let it clog up the negotiations. As an example, the questioner asks, "How much profit are you making if you sell this (old) car to me?" An impudent question and one never asked by an experienced salesperson. A suggested answer, "That is quite irrelevant. It is in your hands to decide what the car is worth to you. That is your decision. The price I ask is mine. That really is all that matters".

It is essential to keep the bargaining going and not to let it be interrupted by a silly or pointless question or comment. Generally such a remark is made to confuse you.

ALWAYS TELL THE TRUTH

This item has already been considered and is mentioned again to bring home its importance.

BE CONFIDENT AND ENTHUSIASTIC

As far as circumstances permit be positive as that will show far better than any other display both confidence and enthusiasm. Learn not to hesitate and not to use too many "ifs" and "buts". Such words tend to break up your reasoning and make you sound uncertain of what you are trying to put over. Keep smiling even when on the back foot. There is nothing that breaks the questioner's nerve more than your confident and enthusiastic answers that leave little room for a positive comeback. A useful guide to remember - a salesperson must be a good actor but his audience must not know that he is acting.

A summary - To be **CONFIDENCE** is being positive, being assured, being bold, being firm, being self-reliant and being reasonable. To be **ENTHUSIASTIC** is being keen, being ardent, being avid, being eager, being fervent, being vigorous and ready, able and willing to get on with the job.

BE CLEAR IN YOUR REPLY TO A QUESTION. YOU MUST NEVER BE MISUNDERSTOOD.

On rare occasions you may feel that it suits the circumstances to be vague. A word of caution is needed here. The questioner will consider that vagueness shows that the question has hit home. So, on all occasions be as clear as possible so that there is no doubt whatsoever that the questioner is not scoring points. As an example, the question asked is this, "How long has the car been for sale?" The honest answer is "For three months", but you mumble, "Not for long". That is both untrue and unclear and will give the questioner confidence that you want to hide the true answer. Hence, his offer is likely to be below what he was thinking before you made that slip. See difficult question number two for more on this subject.

Always be clear and show that you are in complete control of the situation and are willing to answer truthfully all questions posed.

IF YOU CANNOT ANSWER A QUESTION, SAY SO

If you do not have the necessary information and you cannot answer the question there is only one way out. That is to say so and to give the reason why and/or offer to find out the answer and get back to him. The latter offer, if accepted, must be carried out without delay or interest may wane. It is never good policy to give a bald, "Sorry, I don`t know". That response can so easily be misconstrued - what is being hidden? A confident and clear answer is along these lines, "Now, that is a good question. I haven`t thought of that. Let me research and get back to you. I`ll call you tomorrow". If the questioner is keen to do a deal there and then he is likely to continue the negotiations without an answer.

ALWAYS BE REASONABLE

Do not act or speak in an extravagant, immodest or irrational manner. The only way to behave is in your "everyday manner". Trying to impress is likely to upset the applecart, the questioner may retaliate by adopting the same attitude. That will make the negotiations that much more difficult. You must be the everyday you, not an actor trying (too hard) to impress.

ALWAYS REASON, NEVER "BLOW YOUR TOP"

When buying or selling reasoning is being alert, being logical, being calm and, not to be forgotten, really listening to the other person`s point of view. If reasoning becomes a shouting match, a quarrel or a row it is drifting away from compromise and from a satisfactory solution. Reasoning could be defined as being an argument with all the rough edges smoothed away - no shouting of (unpleasant) names, no bullying and no vulgar language...and that is how the most difficult and belligerent person must be treated and answered. Do not let your answer start a quarrel. Let it start a quiet, peaceful and intelligent period of reasoning. If you lose your temper or your humour you are likely to lose the deal or, at best, get a less rewarding settlement. Keep your foot on the "restrain accelerator" and you will speedily be on the way to winning the argument.

DO NOT BRING IN ANY UNRELATED TOPIC

To bring in an unrelated aside will cause both confusion and, to the questioner, it may seem that the question is not being dealt with in the proper manner. This is yet another situation where he may consider that you are trying to avoid a discriminating question by distracting his attention away from the true answer. Make it a rule - one of many rules that you have to learn! - not to gossip, natter, waffle, preach, et al. Keep strictly to a clear and unambiguous answer that really does deal with the question and show that you are strictly on the ball.

DO NOT BE CONTROVERSIAL

Answering most questions will, by its very nature, involve a certain degree of being controversial. That cannot be avoided. Do not bring in to your answer any other controversial topic. For example, do not use the occasion to settle an old score or to boast just to display your intelligence. At best, such a display will go in one of the questioner's ears and out of the other. He will not be interested unless, and here is the danger, he hears something that he can profitably use against you. Again, the advice is to keep an answer clear, simple and directly related to the question and the business in hand. Do not wander off into dangerous contentious grounds.

DO NOT BE TOO CLEVER

This principle and the last one are related and should be considered together.

Each one of us has an aspiration to be known as being clever and intellectually ahead of others. Perhaps it is a human trait that we conceal our (assumed) cleverness behind the proverbial bushel and only display it when it is needed to impress others or to boost our own ego. Be that as it may, it is never the right time to display it when answering a question. By giving a down to earth answer you have achieved your objective. To completely ruin it by adding an aside is both self-defeating and risky. It is likely to annoy the questioner and make him a more difficult person to deal with. So, do not display that cleverness keep it under the bushel. Use it; do not display it. To put that counsel into an expression commonly used - do not show off; that will display a lack of real competence.

DO NOT ATTEMPT TO DISPLAY A FALSE FRONT

The word "attempt" is used to show that putting on a false front rarely works. It is both vain and unproductive to attempt it whilst answering a question. Most questioners will see through your act and realise that the truth is being hidden. As the only reason for putting on a false front is to try to mislead the questioner`s assumption could well be correct. He realises that you are in deep trouble. To be so exposed when you consider that all is going fine is a maximum plus point to the questioner - and, of course, a big minus one to you. He sees a worried person hiding behind a false veneer. You see, you truly gain by being your everyday self - no false front, just the real you.

There are generally exceptions to the harshest rules. As you read this book it will be realised that the salesperson has, at times, to be a first-class actor. That is, of course, true. But, and this is the important point, when you have to act you are NOT putting on a completely false front; you are strengthening a vulnerable position by cleverly displaying both confidence and enthusiasm. This is a completely different feat than putting on a false front. Being an actor is an exercise that can only be fully developed as you tackle real life situations.

IGNORE OPPONENT`S COMPLIMENTS

That may sound brash; unfortunately you will on rare occasions have to be a little offensive. It is too easy to fall for that compliment and drop your guard whilst happily acknowledging it. The questioner is certainly trying to flatter you; to be more precise trying to butter-you-up. He wants you to accept him as a friend and, hence, you can safely deal with him. Forget the compliment and consider all his questions in your usual careful manner. A synonym for "compliment" is "flattery"- that is, insincere praise. Beware! Didn`t Shakespeare tell us that there are certain signs to know faithful friend from flattering foe?

A PRECISE SUMMARY OF THESE GENERAL PRINCIPLES - Let every answer really reply to the question posed and be clear, reasonable and truthful.

A GENERAL SUMMARY - It will not be too difficult to recall these general principles. It will achieve little to rely on learning by rote. By carefully reading and considering each principle you will very soon appreciate what should or should not be said or done. Then, when you negotiate you will instinctively operate without consciously thinking back. There will not be time to recall those principles when in a real life situation. It will be necessary to act very fast. Only by being involved in the real day-to-day process of buying and selling will the correct way to proceed be learnt. Do remember, you learn not so much from successes as from analysing your mistakes.

It does not matter whether you are a person who has his own private residence to sell, a trader who makes a living by buying and selling any item under the sun, a person who occasionally sells an item for which he has no further use, a shopkeeper who is selling each and every day to earn a fair living and so on. The questions that you will be asked will all have the same objective, the same cunning way of trying to extract from you a little - or large! - gem that will assist the questioner. Never forget that without exception every buyer and seller wants to do his best to outdo the opponent. The questions will, of course, vary in wording but the target is always the same. The lesson to be learnt is this - whatever the subject of the negotiation treat each and every question in the same (very) cautious way; do not drop your guard for one moment - always be on alert.

*   *   *   *   *   *

THE FIFTEEN DIFFICULT QUESTIONS

These are heard in all types of markets. Do not dismiss a question as it does not seem to relate to your own sphere of activity. Look at it carefully and endeavour to hear it being asked, probably in different wording. In that way you will realise that whatever you are buying or selling there will be a wide range of difficult questions to answer but, and here is the benefit, you will soon accumulate a useful range of potent answers. Each difficult question will now be considered.

ONE – WHY ARE YOU SELLING?

This is probably the most asked question. It may seem innocent and often is. However, it is used as a way of attempting to ascertain how desperate you are to sell. If you are frantic to sell and you, as they say, spill the beans...well, any offer that you receive will reflect your display of desperation. You will damage - down value - your own asset.

When selling a property you must be careful with your answer for both this and question two can so easily tie you in knots. An example, you are moving to be near a sick relation. If you say exactly that a prospective purchaser is likely to conclude that you want to move pdq - in fact, urgently. He is correct. To avoid that conclusion answer along these lines, "We would like to be nearer Mother". Note: you have not said "sick" or "elderly" as those words could give the impression that a move is urgent. You continue, "We are not tied to any specific timetable. We could move to suit a purchaser". That excellent answer illustrates that you are flexible on timing and will help a purchaser by giving possession when he requires. It takes the emphasis away from you and shows that you are a helpful person and that will be a big plus for you.

With a property sale a problem arises when there is a real urgent reason for selling. For example, you may be under pressure from a bank, be in arrears with your mortgage, owe money to a business associate, et al. The reason must, as far as is possible, remain a personal secret. Your answer could be, "We are going to downsize as the house has become too large for us". If too large is not applicable consider other reasons such as - a difficult journey to work, want to be nearer our best friends, the garden is too large as we are not keen gardeners and so on. You get the drift. The reason may only be partially true but do keep the answer away from finance. If it is known locally that you are in financial trouble you must be strictly honest. Say, "Sadly we have fallen on difficult times. We do want to sell as soon as we can but, of course, we are not going to sell under market value. We have no reason to do that. Our estate agent is advising us on price".

The correct answer must not display any sense of urgency. To do so will be fatal to any offer that you receive. It will be way below the asking price. It is repeated - if at all possible keep the answer well away from finance/money.

Sadly, a white lie may be your only real way out. Nevertheless, do not be tempted to tell a lie that is not feasible or one that could in some way rebound to your detriment.

TWO – HOW LONG HAS IT BEEN ON OFFER?

Like question one the wrong answer can have an adverse effect on any offer that you receive. It stands to reason that the longer an item has been for sale some disabilities will have a bearing on its sale:

Firstly, the item has a defect and that is not reflected in the asking price. Your antique porcelain jug was valued at circa £750 when in pristine condition. Sadly, you chipped it and the valuer reduced the valuation to £400. You did not take his advice and it has been on the market for three months at £650. Reason for lack of sale - the asking price did not reflect the defect.

Secondly, your second-hand car was valued at £5,250. You put it on the market for £6,500 and it has remained unsold for ten weeks. Reason for lack of sale - the asking price is well over true market value.

In the above examples it is your fault that the items are unsold. You are being greedy. However, you now realise that common sense must prevail and are prepared to be realistic. You have now been asked the question and have to deal with it warts and all. There is no way to wipe out the past. You realise that a prospective buyer is more than likely to have seen your abortive advertisements. Your reply relating to the car is along these lines, "I was advised by the local garage that the value of the car is around £5,250. Like us all I was greedy and wanted more. Of course, I couldn`t sell at the higher figure. However, that`s the past and I will now sell at £5,500". Note that you avoid directly answering the question. As his sole objective in asking the question was, no doubt, to pave the way for a price reduction he has succeeded.

If the asking price is about right there is generally only one reason why a sale has not materialised and that is that market conditions are against you. That question is one of the most difficult to answer. As seen in the example in the last paragraph price can be talked down and that, at least on the face of it, is a sound solution. If you reply that the sole reason why the item has not been sold is that market conditions are against you it is implied that the only sensible answer is a reduction in price; of course that would help in a difficult market.

If you are able and willing to await better market conditions - and that is being a true gambler! - a useful answer could be, "I know that business is not very good, nevertheless I am confident that the asking price fully reflects the slowness in business. I am quite happy to await events and I know that I will obtain my price". That is a proud boast and a fine display of confidence - by a not too confident seller!

If you know of a recent sale of a similar item at a comparable price to your asking price do not hesitate to put it before an interested party. The more true examples the better. Such data is convincing and can often help to obtain a sale; it is good evidence that despite current market conditions business is still being transacted. At the very least this evidence will help to boost your own confidence and you will lose that losing look.

When the question is asked and you are selling a house you must be very careful. Your home has been advertised in the local press and the questioner is likely to have seen the displays. The question could be posed to see if you are truthful. Depending on the circumstances and your wish to always be honest here are some suggested answers - "It has been on the market at a higher price. It was reduced to its present price only three days ago", "Our new home was not available to move into so we asked the estate agents not to push this property. You know what estate agents are like - they rarely listen", "We spend some three weeks talking to a prospective buyer. He had to withdraw as his own sale fell through. I suppose we were silly to wait but he seemed so genuine" and so on. As a last resort consider being really truthful, "The estate agents are as puzzled as we are. They say the price is right. We took their advice. Maybe we are just unlucky".

The correct answer is to always tell the truth - or, at worse, do not get too far away from it! Possibly "gild the lily" just a little as the above answers suggest. You must give a feasible answer or else saleability will be greatly reduced. Make your answer and the way it is said show complete confidence and, thus, help to give an uplift to the questioner's desire.

THREE – HOW MUCH DID IT COST YOU?

When selling most items this is a comparatively easy question to avoid. You do not answer as it is a cheeky question and is commonly used to try to ascertain your profit margin. With that information the prospective buyer can pitch an offer to give you what he considers a fair profit. It is not his job to fix the profit. Some persons just hate to give another person a profit and that is just plain silly. They ought to concern themselves with making sure that they purchase at today's value or less. That is the buyer's true job.

Your best course of action is to kill the question immediately with these words, "That information will not be of any use to you. I am selling TODAY and, of course, am asking the price it is worth today. It is up to you to decide its worth to you". Give a polite and yet firm non-answer. That is all that you need say.

When selling a property the scenario is entirely different. Do not forget that recent sale prices are on the Internet and, therefore, know to one and all. There are few secrets. If a prospective purchaser mentions your historic purchase price say, "We are selling and buying on today`s market. Prices go up and down. The asking price is as advised by our estate agent who is, of course, completely in touch with property values in this area. Our asking price is a sensible today`s value". An answer along those lines seeks to get the conversation back to today`s prices and emphasises that the asking price was advised by a qualified person.

If money has been spent on the property during your ownership the price that you paid becomes even less relevant. For some illogical reason that state of affairs impels many interested parties to believe that you are a property developer and seeking to make a good profit. They become determined to know what the property cost and the amount of money spent on improvements. Politely and firmly ignore their questions and say, "When we bought the property it was very rundown and we have improved it. We didn`t do the work to make money. Our only consideration was to have a comfortable home for the family. The next occupier will enjoy all our hard work". That answer concentrates on what the house is now - a home ready to move into.

The correct answer is to move away from the past and get the questioner thinking about today, especially today`s values. Get him thinking about the present day value of your house and, also, the suitability of it for his family.

FOUR – ARE THERE ANY PROBLEMS?

The curt and ill-mannered answer is that it is the questioner`s job to find that out. That is the truth. However, you should never be so blunt and it is the one occasion when you endeavour, if needs be, to avoid the truth!

Unless the goods or chattels being sold are in some way defective or in poor general condition all you need say is, "Well, there is the dining room suite. Please do inspect it thoroughly - don`t take my word for it." That answer puts the onus on the questioner. A word of warning - do bear in mind that that answer should only be given when you are sure that the item is in good condition. Otherwise any flaw is likely to be found and that will make the asking price very suspect. "Wasn't your price for a suite in good order...and didn't you invite me to inspect it? Were you really confident or just hoping that the wonky leg to one of the dining chairs would not be noticed?" You should not take such a risk; you gambled and lost. You are now in deep trouble. Also, as you seemed to imply that the item was in good condition you will, if the viewer is still interested, receive a lower offer.

If the item has a defect and you priced accordingly you are on firmer ground. Indicate the defect before it is found by the viewer. You say, "As you see there is a small crack on one of the cups. The other five are perfect. That is why I am asking £200 for the set - well below the value of a set in perfect condition". Make him realise the difference in price between "perfect" and "not quite perfect" and impress that he is being offered a first-rate deal. Also, disclose the expert who gave you the values.

When a house is being sold the situation can become more difficult. The asking price had been agreed with your estate agent; it is probably today's value plus something to bargain with when negotiations commence. It will - or should - reflect all known defects - such as poor decorations, old central heating system, out-of-date kitchen and bathroom, traffic noise from the main road and so on. The answer to the question is this, "Our estate agent advised on price. We accepted that advice and it does reflect that certain improvements are needed. You can see where improvements are needed. I do not know of any other problems". That is a truthful answer.

However, as is often the case when selling a house problems do arise. The house is sold, subject to contract, and along comes a Chartered Surveyor who finds some faults that you did not know existed. Maybe it is some dry rot in the basement playroom, an opening between the lounge and dining room should be spanned by an RSJ, some slight settlement in the front bay and so on. The prospective purchaser come s along with a lower offer as advised by his Chartered Surveyor. Do not get involved in such complicated dealings. Your estate agent and other professional advisers will have to advise you (1) If the Chartered Surveyor's report is correct - or partially correct? (2) What is the cost of correcting any defects? Then, with all the necessary advice in hand you will be able to decide whether to reduce the agreed price or to carry out the works to remedy the defects and put the house back on the market at the then value. Those alternatives raise many questions that have to be discussed and answered before a decision is taken and are beyond the scope of this book. This paragraph illustrates that in some specific circumstances relating to property you cannot answer a question without taking professional advice.

In all cases the correct answer is that you are fully aware that the item is not perfect and the asking price reflects its existing state. You must stress that last statement and if possible hammer home the true value in a perfect state. Let the prospective purchaser see the difference. You must realise that the top price will not be obtained for even a slightly damaged article. Likewise, a prospective purchaser must realise - and be told in no uncertain terms - that he must pay the price taking into account any damage. You must both be realistic.

This question and the various answers apply to antiques and paintings. It is an important aspect of selling or buying such items that expert advice should always be taken.

FIVE – ARE YOU SURE THAT IT`S BY...? WHO ADVISED YOU?

These two questions are so related that they are best treated as one. Both are generally only asked when antiques, paintings and collectables are offered for sale. To be able to correctly identify the creator or painter of an article has an exceptional effect on its value. You know - or believe you know - that the item being sold is genuine. Nevertheless, to get the top price you may have to prove it. An example, an old Worcester coffee cup was the only item of value that your Mother left you. Sadly, times are hard and it must be sold. The distinguishing marks on the cup are unreadable but you trusted your mother`s judgement and you know that it is really old Worcester. It is on offer for £150 and is in perfect condition. You are asked the two questions and the suggested answers are as follows:

Firstly, you have no real evidence. You merely replied that it had been in the family for many years and was always considered to be old Worcester. The questioner pushes you - you have no firmer evidence. The unreadable distinguishing marks do not help. As a result the asking price is beginning to look well over the top. You "valued" the cup by looking at antiques for sale on the Internet. Old Worcester porcelain seemed quite sought-after. You are beginning to wish that you had more trustworthy evidence. You urgently need some cash and say, "I am convinced that it is old Worcester. It has been in the family for many years. However, I agree that the marks are not readable and there is no other evidence. I`ll accept £125 and that`s my lowest". This is a case where you have been caught out because you went into a negotiation completely unprepared. Your evidence was, to say the least, flimsy.

Secondly, before offering the cup for sale you took expert advice. It was confirmed that it was a Worcester coffee cup circa 1780 and worth circa £200. When the two questions were asked you had the perfect answers with an expert`s written opinion. You were asking £230 and because of the evidence you realised that price. You were well rewarded for anticipating the questions. The lesson to be learnt is this - some questions are so obvious that, even before being asked, you are able to put together a truthful and, to you, profitable answer. This is another example of careful preparation bring success.

The provenance of an item is of great help when answering a hostile question. The history is not only of interest, it can also help to add to the evidence that a painting is really a Picasso...and not a fake! To use that type of information when answering a question is a great plus to you.

The correct answer can, as previously stated, be prepared before the question is asked. It does not take a genius to realise that those two wily questions will be throw at you. The correct evidence (provenance) will help to convince the questioner and, therefore, it is not a waste of time going to a lot of trouble to obtain it. That may prove that the painting is truly a Picasso...and that will depress any questioner and open his purse.

Those two questions can only be convincingly answered when the correct evidence has been assembled and is readily available to put before the questioner. The questions illustrate how vital it is to do proper research when proposing to sell an antique, painting or a collectable - by doing so you add value.

SIX – DON`T YOU AGREE THAT YOUR ASKING PRICE IS TOO HIGH?

Always be cautious when dealing with a person who tries to put words into your mouth.

Before answering this question it will be useful to consider how you should arrive at an asking price. If the article is an everyday object easy to price or an expert`s opinion has been obtained you have no worries. You can prove with confidence its true value. If on the other hand, you guessed the price or took and would not accept an expert`s valuation you could be heading for trouble.

Firstly, you are confident that the asking price is about right. You reply, "I know from the experience of this marketplace that my asking price is not too high and is realistic and compares favourably with similar items now being offered. I took a lot of trouble to get the price right as I am a willing seller at a sensible price. I am not someone who will sell only at an over the top price".

Alternatively to the above reply, if available you produce the expert`s valuation which, to a certain extent, speaks for itself. Of course, that valuation can always be challenged; then if you have complete confidence in it that confirms your answer to the question.

Secondly, when you have either tested the market for several weeks and have not sold or because after discussions with a prospective buyer or two you have to admit to yourself that you have overestimated the market value. If you have not brought the price down to a sensible level you answer the question by saying. "I may have **slightly** overestimated the value". Note, the use of the word "slightly". That reply is a short, neat and diplomatic way of implying that you are asking for a close offer on the asking price; not, of course, a silly offer as the asking price is only "slightly" over true market value. OK, you cannot stop an interested party making a silly offer but, at least, that could start negotiations.

If you will only sell at a price well over market value you must be perfectly frank. You have no evidence to support the asking price

- none exists - and you realise that there is plenty of evidence to undermine it. In those circumstances there is only one answer. You say, "I don't want to waste your time. I will only sell at my asking price. I am not interested in any offers. I am being straight with you. It is up to you to make a decision. There is no point in trying to negotiate". The disappointed prospective purchaser is more than likely to walk away. As you would (definitely) not sell at less than the asking price you are not unhappy.

It might be good policy to add to the answer given in the last paragraph words to the effect that you are offering really good value and, more to the point, it is an item that will show good value appreciation in the future. That is a bit wishy-washy; nevertheless, the purchaser may weaken. It is important that when selling you always remain the super optimistic salesperson.

The correct answer to this difficult question is to display a bold front. If you are compelled to admit that the asking price is high qualify your answer by using the word "slightly" or similar. It is always an advantage to possess an expert's written opinion when dealing with an antique or a pictures. When dealing with property refer the question to the estate agent and explain that they advised you on value and are, of course, the experts.

SEVEN – DO YOU REALISE I CAN BUY CHEAPER ELSEWHERE?

The simple answer is, "Then, why don't you do so?" However, that is an impolite answer. This is a question that is best answered by asking questions rather than by giving a poor rambling reply.

It stands to reason that if the questioner really knew where he could buy a similar item at a lower price he would not waste time talking to you. Therefore, there must be a reason why the question is being asked. He could be a bad negotiator just trying it on and hoping that the question will flummox you and that the asking price will be quickly reduced. You so he (wrongly) thinks will rush to do a deal before he buys elsewhere. The writer is reminded off an apt quotation from Julius Caesar, "There is no terror, Cassius, in your threats" and those are your thoughts as you reflect on the question. You should deal with the question as suggested in the next paragraph.

It could be that the truth is being only partially told. The item seen elsewhere is in poor condition or has some defect. It is not easy to get an admission to that effect. If the item is a valuable one - say, a car - make an outright and rather cheeky challenge, "Now, that is very interesting. I would love to see it. Will you take me to it?" Now, that is a real dare. It is unlikely that the challenge will be taken up. He hesitates. You continue, "Perhaps the car isn't in such good condition as mine...or, older?" He huffs and puffs. You tease him, "If it's cheaper and in better condition than mine I may want to buy it. Come on, let's go and see it". Finally you realise that there is no hope of the challenge being taken up. At the appropriate time you bring the chat about the phantom car to a close. You say, "I will not comment on a car I haven't seen. You won't let me see it, so let's get down to brass tacks and concentrate on **MY** car...would you like a test drive?" The questioner must be pushed into a position where he will be greatly relieved to forget the other car and will realise that he has been rumbled. Your questions did the trick - his clumsy ploy has failed.

It will never be known with any certainty whether or not the competing item existed. However, by asking probing questions and asking to see that item you will get some idea as to whether or not the truth is being told. In fact, its existence does not matter as you treat both the truth and a lie with the same probing manner. It will be a new ball game if your challenge to see the other item is taken up. Then, a true comparison can take place and that, as they say, is another story.

With property this question is easier to answer. True comparisons are likely to be in the area or in similar residential areas of the town. With your estate agent's help you have researched the town and are likely to know if any similar houses on the market are of better value that yours. In fact, being a (true) willing seller you have endeavoured to be offering the very best value in the town. Answer the question by asking one, "Which house or houses have you in mind and which have you inspected internally?" You should be able to comment on any house mentioned in answer to those questions. You will quickly remember all bad points! If you feel that you are losing the argument refer the questioner to your estate agent.

The correct answer to this question is to keep asking questions about the (assumed) other item. Do not give up. Get the questioner in a position where he is eager to forget the dicey comparison and desperate to talk about the real item. That will be a plus point for you.

EIGHT – DO YOU REALISE THAT THERE IS LITTLE DEMAND TODAY FOR...?

A dealer friend of mine always starts his sales patter by saying, "No one is buying that stuff today". He is adamant and will rarely listen to reason. Despite that negative approach he prospers. He is a full-time dealer and sees many items each week and can afford to miss out on some. Many sellers fall for his patter and he buys many realistically priced items. He causes some sellers to panic and grab a lower price rather than run the risk of not selling. Overall his plan works. You will have noticed that he does not ask a question. He awaits the sellers reply and hopes that his opening remarks are accepted as a fact. If you face a buyer who uses a similar opening remark deal with him as though he has asked a question. The implied question is this - by how much will you reduce the asking price in order to sell your out-of-date item?"

There are two ways to answer this awkward start. You can be positive, brush aside the remark and keep praising your goods in the usual way or be jovial and politely call him a typical dealer. Proceed as follows:

Firstly, you praise your goods and their excellent value. If you are a dealer you say, "Knowing the market as I do my goods are saleable and priced to sell - warts and all. I have been in this business for fourteen years and don`t waste my time by marketing unsaleable goods". If you are a private seller you say, "I am sure that you are not right. I did some research before putting the goods on the market and found no evidence whatsoever that they are outdated. These are saleable goods at a realistic price. If you think contrary I won`t waste time I`ll go elsewhere". In either case you take the initiative. No "ifs" and no "buts" for you have no doubt there is a demand. Shoot him down before his pessimism shoots you down.

Secondly, take a risk that the dealer has a sense of humour. Give a bright smile and say, "Most dealers start just like that. It`s your attempt to start the ball rolling towards a lower price. Come on, let`s get real and down to business". Alternatively say, "OK, I know all about that. You hope to buy well under value, then straight back to your villa in Bermuda. Come on, let`s get down to brass tacks. I know that my goods are saleable…and so do you". Quite often a little jovial dig will produce a realistic attitude in even the most hard-hearted dealer. He sees a seller who does not cave in to his patter.

The correct answer to this question is to immediately accept the challenge and fight back. In both of the above answers be positive and do not give even a slight hint that he may be right. To add that you have researched the market or taken an expert`s advice will indicate that you are confident. If he sticks to his view start asking questions and commence with, "Why do you say that my goods are not in demand? Please give me your evidence". Keep pushing for evidence and do not be satisfied with hearsays. He may be hard pushed to give any real evidence. You are likely to find that his words were thrown at you without any shrewd thinking. He was starting to deal in his zombie-like manner. He may catch some sellers - but he won`t catch you. Always remember this warning - once a dealer always a dealer.

NINE – DON`T YOU AGREE THAT THE RECESSION IS HAVING A MARKED LOWERING EFFECT ON PRICES?

You can argue for a long time about your asking price. In the final analysis it is a subjective concept. Seller and buyer each have their own opinion. That gives two uncertainties - the circumstances and the price. In this question both are prime factors. It is possible that the questioner sees - or, hopes that the seller will see - a recession with a downward influence on prices generally. There are two situations to consider:

Firstly, when the questioner is referring to a mild slowdown in commerce as a recession to frighten the seller into accepting a very low offer you say, "There is only a mild slowdown in specific areas of the economy. Certainly nowhere near a real recession. I have priced my goods somewhat lower in price that I was obtaining three or so months ago. That reduction more than reflects the **slight** slowdown in the market". Note (again!) the use of the word "slight" and, also, "specific" for they help to show that you do not agree with the question and that any slowdown in business is minimal. You are talking his recession down to a slight slowdown in specific sections of the economy. That is far from a true recession and you hope that he will realise that he cannot fool you with his totally wrong assumption.

Consider if there is no slowdown in business and it is just a pious hope in a bad negotiator`s attempt to frighten you and to get the asking price down; then you can take one of the following lines of reasoning. "Now, that`s interesting. I haven`t heard that from any other source. What is your evidence, please?", or, "Oh, that`s news to me. Please explain". Calmly and politely embarrass him and he will soon realise that he has been rumbled and that he is wrongly pushing a phantom recession.

Secondly, when a damaging recession is harming business and there is no doubt whatsoever that prices are (nearly) in free fall. The question is difficult to answer in those indisputable circumstances. However, the true salesperson is rarely beaten. This is another situation where you use both price and quality to answer a difficult question. You say, "Of course we are all suffering. I realise that prices **have** fallen. That is why I have carefully priced so as to be in line with today`s values. I can`t beat the market so to compete I offer first-class goods at today`s prices. It would be silly for me to do otherwise". Note the emphasis on "**have** fallen" - that gives a better impression than saying "are falling" as that would put your asking price at further risk.

A private seller would have to fall back on the care taken when pricing. Say, "I have spoken to two experts who know the value of such items. I took their advice as they, more than I, know the effect of the recession on prices". If at all possible have up-to-the-minute written evidence, although that is difficult if you have a value from an elderly lady in the corner shop!

With houses there is evidence of a recession for all to see. There are many more For Sale boards on display and lower prices in advertisements. You can deal with the question by saying, "The asking price is as advised by our estate agents and, of course, they know the ruling prices. Mr Brown, who is dealing with our affairs, will be able to discuss today`s conditions and prices with you. Why not give him a call". Any evidence that you have of recent sales in your immediate area will be useful information to give to viewers.

The correct answer to this difficult question is never to be intimidated by the questioner. Fight back by convincing him that the price was fixed by taking into account all of today`s conditions and, of course, you are fully aware that conditions are not ideal - that is why you were careful not to get optimistic. You are a seller at today`s price.

TEN – HAVE YOU ANY OTHER INTEREST OR RECEIVED ANY OFFERS?

This question is often asked when you are selling a house. If you are bold - and reckless - you will reply that you have a person who is keen and that you anticipate an offer very soon. Whether or not that is the truth it is not the correct way to answer that question. There is a possibility that it may encourage the viewer to make a quick decision but it is more likely to dampen his enthusiasm as he does not want to compete and force the price higher. Before considering how to answer it must be clearly understood that in no circumstances should you disclose any dealings with other possible buyers. Never boast of real or fictitious interest. Do not frighten a possible buyer away.

Firstly, when you really have no other interest the least said the better. But, of course, you cannot remain silent and must reply in some way. Say, "I have other viewers who, I believe, are going to see the estate agent". That is a vague yet suitable answer and gives nothing away. It is honest as there have been other viewers who might or might not see the estate agents. If the house has only been on the market for a few days say, "Didn`t the estate agents tell you that we only went onto the market last Friday. You are our first viewer".

Secondly, when you have genuine interest from viewers you reply, "Yes, we have other viewers who are in touch with the estate agents and suggest that you, also, call and see them". If you are pushed say no more and repeat that a call on the estate agents would be the best course of action. To reply in that manner does not involve going into greater detail; let the estate agents do that. They are experts at negotiating - let them earn their commission!

With items other than houses adopt a similar low-key attitude. You are alone and it is your job to do the negotiating. The item being sold is yours; the price has been quoted. Let the prospective buyer talk. When forced to answer the question say, "The item is now available for sale. It is in your hands as to whether or not it suits your needs. Come on, let's get down to business and do a deal now". The answer ignores the question. Alternatively, if the questioner is a friendly type say, "Ah...now that would be telling...the item is here and you can buy it **now**". That simple answer is likely to be construed that he must hurry or lose out to another person. That is what you intended the question to imply - your friendly answer was the correct one.

The correct answer is not to boast of any offers or other interest. Give the direct answer that the goods are there to be purchased **now**. You want to increase his interest, not deflate it.

ELEVEN – WHAT PRICE WILL YOU ACCEPT?

This absurd question makes me very angry. The answer that I want to give is, "Do you expect me to do your work for you? I can't be buyer and seller. You know the price that I am asking. Don't you know how to negotiate?" But one must never be rude, appear to be angry or a clever dick. In any event that answer would not help negotiations. Often, I rather cheekily reply with the asking price for, after all, that is the price that I would accept. Ask a silly question and you get a sensible answer!

A more realistic reply is along these lines, "As you know I am asking £1,000. It is not a priced guessed by me. It is not a starting price. I have been advised by an expert on Doulton figurines that I should obtain £1,000 for it. You see, my asking price is based on an expert's opinion of value". Those words, like all the answers given in this book, can be altered to suit circumstances.

At antique fairs it is the custom to ask, "What's your best?"

Well, when in Roman do as the Romans do. However, in most cases the asking price includes a little extra so that the question can be answered positively. "Oh, to you...£120."... and, of course, to anyone else.

Conversely, when buying I rarely ask this question. It is the buyer's job to use his experience and guile to get the price reduced - or, at least - to try to obtain a reduction. If asked and the seller replies with a figure, that figure become a firm price in the seller's mind. Sadly, the difficult question has produced a reply and, to the prospective buyer's detriment may have concentrated the seller's mind on that figure. Having retreated to that given figure he will retreat no further. That low, no lower. So, never ask that difficult question - negotiate.

The correct answer to this difficult question is, once again, to avoid a direct reply. Put clearly before the questioner the exceptional value that you are offering. When a property is involved the only answer is that all aspects of pricing are being dealt with by the estate agent.

TWELVE – I`ll GIVE YOU £X – DON`T YOU AGREE THAT IS A GOOD OFFER?

In this example the questioner is endeavouring to bounce you into agreeing that his offer is a good one. He gives you no time to consider it. He hopes that you will agree and that `s that - a quick deal done. He is working on the basis that many persons go for the easy way and hate to argue or disagree. He may be right but not when you are concerned! However, you must answer; silence or avoidance may be taken as consent and, possibly, used against you later on in the negotiations. Then you will be told, "...but you agreed that my offer was a good one. Are you going back on that assumption?" To avoid that rebuke you must deal with that part of his question before getting down to price. Say, "I could answer your question by **asking you** a question. I could say, `don`t you agree that your offer is a poor one`...you see that style of questioning will get us nowhere". Alternatively, your response could be, "Let`s concentrate on value...and I will let you know when you make an offer that is a good one". That is a little comical and neatly deals with his attempt to put words into your mouth.

In the right circumstances when you feel that the questioner is a person who can take a joke it can be a good ploy to use just a little comedy. Such a response may help to keep the general mood of the meeting at an acceptable genial level. But, do always abide by this rule - never be personal, rude or make any joke at the questioner's expense.

Occasionally you will meet the most annoying person who constantly endeavours to trap you into agreeing with negative questions - those that can only be honestly answered by putting you at a great disadvantage. You will have to be a little aggressive yourself and reply, "Come on, let's be sensible. You keep trying to put words into my mouth. You won't gain by using those tactics. You must realise that I wasn't born yesterday". Sentiments such as those should stop the flow of negative questions and normal negotiations can proceed.

Returning to the implied question - "...you should accept my good offer". It is crucial that you are not bullied by a questioner's attempt to coerce you into agreeing with a statement he has just uttered. Be very careful. Watch for questions that include "...don't you agree?", "...we all know that...", "...it goes without saying...", "...let's be honest..." and so on. You cannot remain silent; you must deal with the comment as outlined above.

The correct way to deal with this difficult question is not to answer the "...don't you agree...?" part of the question with a "yes" or even a "maybe" and do not imply either of those replies. If you get caught and agree your negotiating stance will suffer. Deal with the comment by getting the discussion back to your asking price. However, if it becomes essential that you are obliged to comment on the offer simply say, "Thank you for your offer of £X. It is not acceptable. You know the asking price and your offer is too far away from that". The last sentence does hint that you may consider an offer a little below the asking price. You are endeavouring to get and keep negotiations moving to a successful conclusion.

THIRTEEN – WILL YOU GIVE ME A DAY OR TWO TO CONSIDER?

The only reply is, "Yes, of course. You consider if you want to buy, but I reserve the right to sell elsewhere". In that reply you assume that he is not asking for a day or two to consider and that all other possible interested parties are frozen out. There is no doubt that that is his intension and you have already shot it down in a short and polite fashion.

A more competent questioner will be precise and say, "Will you not sell for two days whilst I consider a purchase. I`ll `phone you at noon on Tuesday". If you answer "yes, of course" you are tending to honour that pledge and giving the questioner a free option on your goods. He may be genuinely undecided and wants a little time to collect his thoughts. That is reasonable but why should you commit yourself when he is unwilling to do so? On the other hand, his question may be a ploy as he is negotiating with another seller for similar goods and is trying to play one seller against another. As you may soon find out he is seeking the cheapest purchase. You may have another purchaser who comes along in the "free option period" and genuinely wants to buy. What will you do if that happens - break your promise and ditch the undecided person. You want to avoid such an unpleasant scenario and, even more so, you want to sell your goods as soon as possible.

The correct answer to safeguard your interest is along these lines, "I would like to help you but I don`t want to lose a sale whilst you consider whether to buy or not". You could add, "I`m here to sell **now**...make a decision now and we will do a deal now. That`s fair...isn`t it?" That is a neat way of putting the ball firmly back into his court. Get him to realise that if he thinks about buying for a day or so he could easily lose out to another buyer.

With a sale of a house the question is not answered as the questioner is referred to the estate agent. Say, "I understand what you are saying. The estate agent is the person to speak to as he is my adviser and is doing all the negotiations on my behalf. Do call and see him". It is extremely unlikely that the estate agent will, on your behalf, give any person a "free option period". He may talk him into making an offer there and then so that he does not lose the property.

FOURTEEN – I`M LOWERING MY OFFER?

This is not a straight question, it is the difficult statement that seller`s dread. It is not because it has to be answered; it is because it could mean a sale at a lower price than originally agreed. The implied threat is that the seller must further reduce the price or the deal is off. This is an occasion when you must not show any sign that you may possibly (slightly) reduce the price so as to obtain a speedy sale. Be confident. Be positive. You have right on your side - although that will not be of any use if you do not play your cards correctly and get the sale reinstated at the original price.

This observation is rarely spoken in just four words. A clever buyer will give the reason - real or make believe - why the offer is being lowered. That will be of great interest to you. However, this is the nub of the way to deal with this tricky person; never get into a discussion on the "why" before you have completely failed to get him to return to the original deal. If you do you are by implication tending to admit that somewhere in the back of your mind you are just beginning to consider a deal at the lower price.

Firstly, with virtually all goods/items except property it is not common for a purchaser to renege on a deal as true reasons for reductions are few and far between. The items have been inspected and, where necessary, professional advice taken and, if a car is involved, it has been test driven. So, there is very little to argue about. Nevertheless, some persons will try it on and have a last fling at getting a few pounds or so off the already agreed price. You must be adamant, you are not going to give the buyer the satisfaction of knowing that a weak you has caved in. You say, "Now that`s odd. I was just going to contact you and say that I have very reluctantly decided that I am selling too cheaply and I want an increase in price". He will be flabbergasted and, probably, lost for words. He will gabble away, "...you can`t do that...we agreed..." You politely point out that what is good for the goose is good for the gander. Then, there is the possibility that you will both agree to conclude the deal at the original price.

If that manoeuvre does not work it maybe that there is a

genuine reason why the price should be reduced. Ask for a detailed explanation. Question him on it. You may arrive at a point where (1) you accept that the reason is genuine and must decide whether to accept the reduced offer, endeavour to negotiate a slightly higher price or remarket the goods and hope that the next prospective buyer is not so observant. Or, (2) decide that the reason for the reduction is not genuine and stand by the original price. Of course, there is always the nonsense of "let's split the difference" but before making any decision do consider the following:

Firstly, mull over the following question - is the reason for the reduced offer relating to the item itself? It should not be so as the prospective buyer was given every opportunity to examine in detail the item and, where applicable, to have it inspected and valued by an expert. So, there is no valid reason for a price reduction unless some genuine new problem has been discovered. This is only likely to happen with antiques, painting and similar. If those circumstances do arise you must, unless you have originally done so, take expert's advice and depending on that advice decide whether or not a price reduction is necessary. You must get together all the facts - the final decision is yours.

Secondly, if the reason is personal to the prospective buyer - for example, the HP company will not advance the required loan on the car, the yearly insurance premiums are much higher than anticipated, the cost of berthing the boat is too high and so on. These are all reasons - or excuses - for the reduced offer. Without any discussion you will say "You should have ascertained all expenses and the like before agreeing to buy". Yes, that comment sounds fair but it does not solve the problem. You are being asked to forego some cash to suit **his** circumstances. It is unfair - but life is unfair and we all have to find ways round difficult problems that are always cropping up. So, at the end of the day it is in your court. Do you want a definite sale now at the reduced price - or, a little higher if you can get it or are you prepared (and happy) to risk market conditions and start seeking a buyer all over again. Only hindsight will confirm whether your judgement was right or wrong. Sadly and unfairly the prospective purchaser has you at his mercy - but, even so, you have the satisfaction of doing what is acceptable to you.

When faced with this difficult question the correct approach is to get all the facts from the questioner before considering the revised offer. Even if the reason for the reduction is an acceptable one the final decision is yours. You must ask yourself this question - will I obtain the agreed price if I remarket? That, to you, is the only consideration that matters; you want to sell at the best possible price. Do always remember that the reason for the reduction must be fully examined as it is likely to have a bearing on any further negotiations.

FIFTEEN – SORRY, BUT I CAN`T PROCEED

There is very little that you can say to an abortive buyer except, goodbye! It is essential to ascertain the exact reason why he is not proceeding. You will have to remarket your possession and when asked why a previous sale did not proceed you must be able to give a genuine answer. This particularly applies to house sale. News travels fast - bad news travels even faster. It will not be easy to keep from other parties the unpleasant fact that a sale has just been lost. Be prepared with the true reason why the sale did not proceed and that will get that difficult out-of-the-way without any harm to you.

*   *   *   *   *   *   *   *

KEEP LEARNING...You must remember that the answers given to these fifteen difficult questions are my guide replies. You must tailor answers to the circumstances of real life situations and with the guidance given in this book you should never be at a loss for an answer. Synonyms of "difficult" include complicated, demanding, onerous, arduous, burdensome, painful and so on. Those words will impress upon you that you must keep learning to deal with all those difficult questions otherwise very many of your negotiations will be unrewarding.

**

www.ingramcontent.com/pod-product-compliance
Lightning Source LLC
Chambersburg PA
CBHW070726180526
45167CB00004B/1634